A true story from the Bible

T0418002

JOSHUA
and the very
STRONG
CiTY

· WRITTEN BY ·
Tim Thornborough

· ILLUSTRATED BY ·
Jennifer Davison

Joshua and the Very Strong City © The Good Book Company, 2025.
Words by Tim Thornborough. Illustrations by Jennifer Davison. Design and art direction by André Parker.

thegoodbook.com • thegoodbook.co.uk • thegoodbook.com.au • thegoodbook.co.nz • thegoodbook.co.in
ISBN: 9781802541250 | JOB-007939 | Printed in India

When soldiers march, their feet make a lot of noise.
In this true story from the Bible, we will be marching
with God's people around a Very Strong City called
Jericho and getting ready to blow our trumpets —
but only when we are told to!

Before we start, let's practise being a marching soldier.

Put on your marching boots.

Get your trumpets ready.

Start to march in time with each other —

Tramp, trampety, tramp, tramp...
Stamp, stampety, stamp, stamp...

but ONLY blow the trumpet when the order is given.

Now you're ready! I hope you enjoy joining Joshua as he
tramps and stamps around Jericho!

Tramp, trampety, tramp, tramp.
Stamp, stampety, stamp, stamp.

Tramp, trampety, tramp, tramp.
Stamp, stampety, stamp, stamp.

Trumpets at the ready!
Stand by to shout!
Deep breath in and...

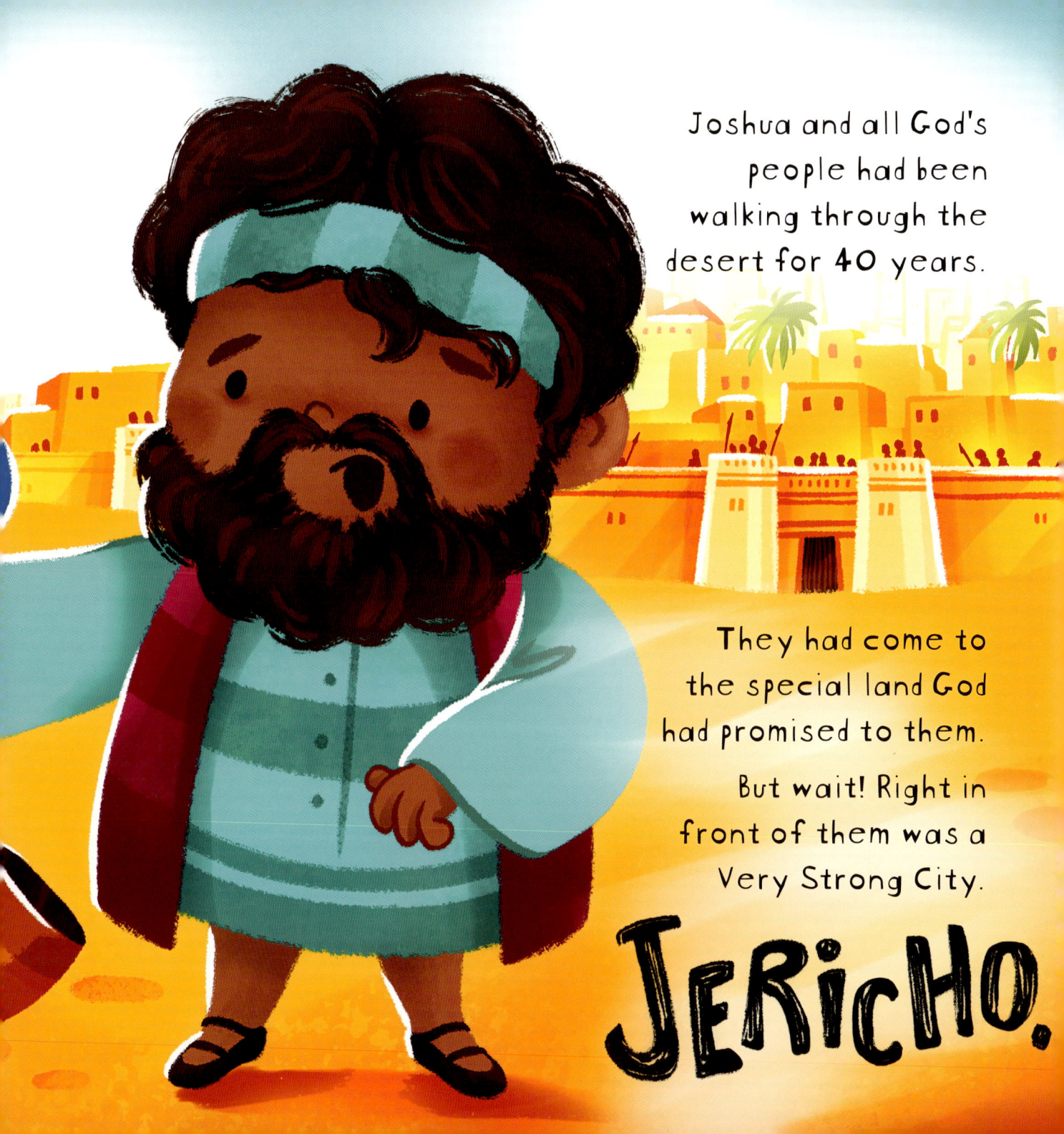

Joshua and all God's people had been walking through the desert for 40 years.

They had come to the special land God had promised to them.

But wait! Right in front of them was a Very Strong City.

JERICHO.

The walls were thick and strong.
The soldiers in Jericho were fierce.

There was no way in and Joshua was worried.

How could they take the Very Strong City and live in the land God had given them?

That night, God gave Joshua some very careful instructions — and a very special promise.

"March around the Very Strong City every day for one, two, three, four, five, six days... but don't blow the big trumpet or shout — you must keep quiet.

"But on day seven, march around the city seven times, and then blow the trumpet and shout. I will give you victory!"

Then the Lord gave Joshua
this very special promise:

"BE STRONG AND BRAVE."

"I am fighting for you.
I will be with you."

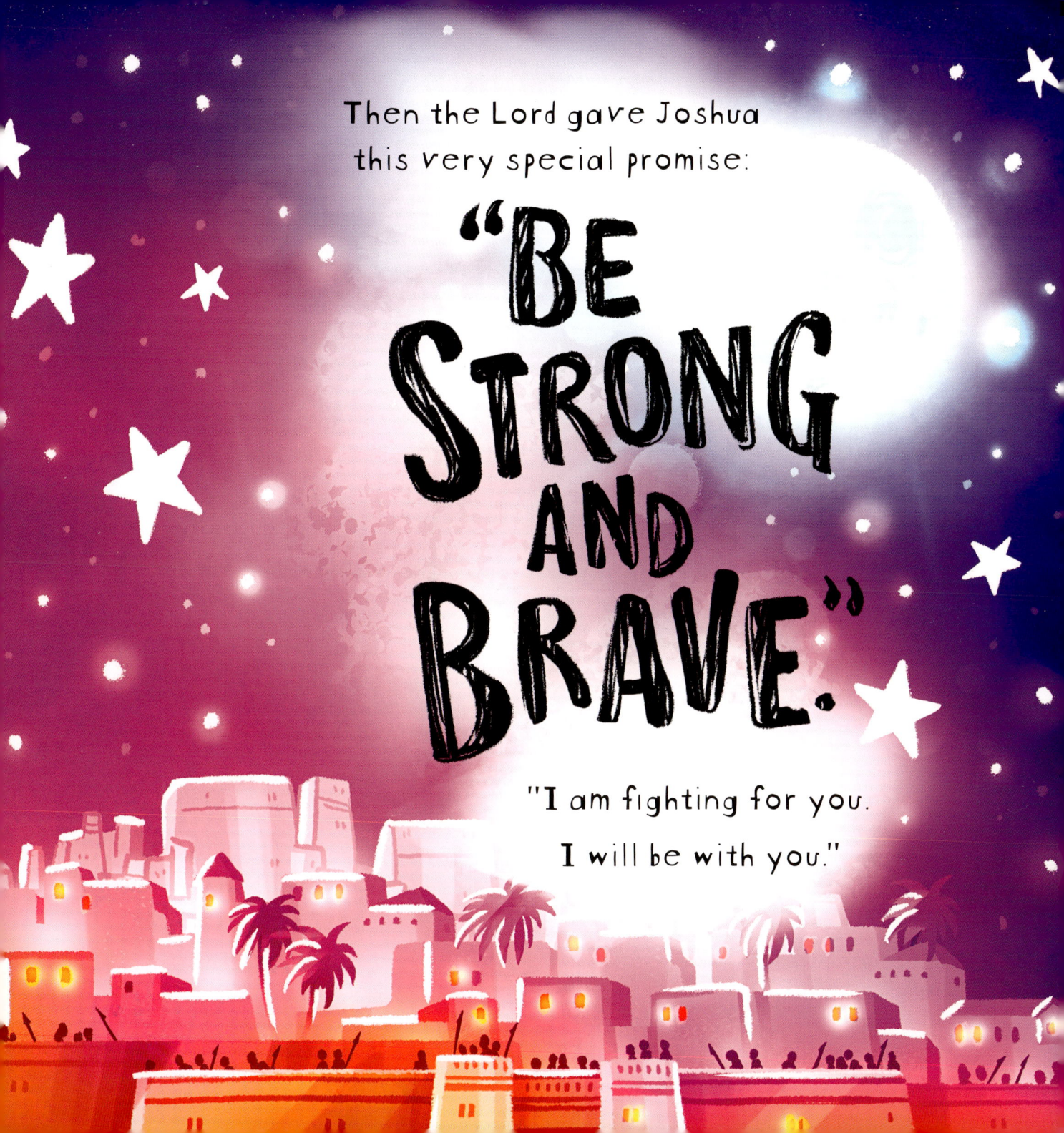

So the next day, Joshua and all of God's people did what God had told them to...

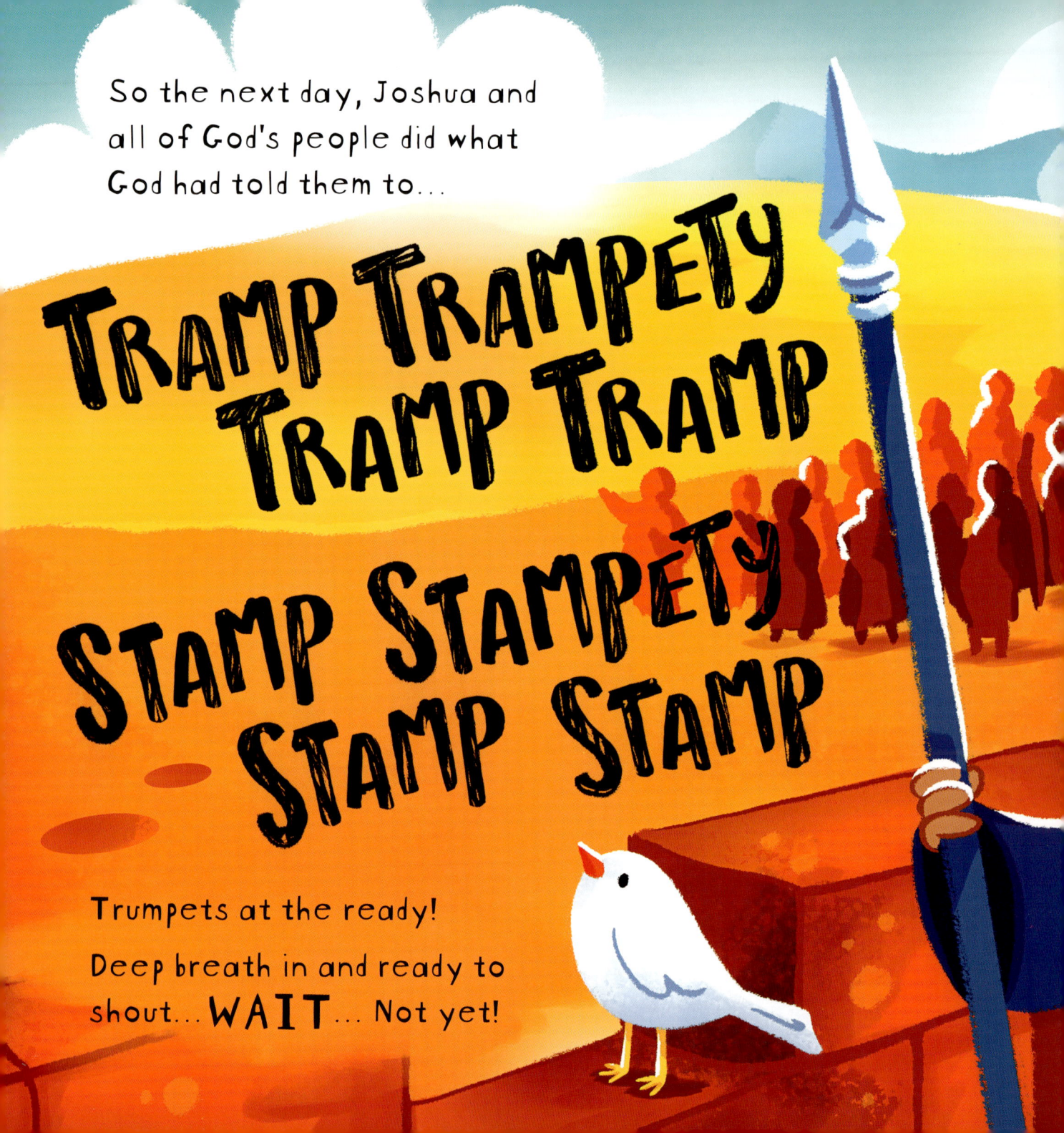

Tramp Trampety Tramp Tramp

Stamp Stampety Stamp Stamp

Trumpets at the ready!
Deep breath in and ready to shout... WAIT... Not yet!

They did this for one, two, three, four, five, SIX DAYS. Then day seven came.

God's people marched round and round the Very Strong City.

Tramp, trampety, tramp, tramp.
Stamp, stampety, stamp, stamp.
(That's once.)

Tramp, trampety, tramp, tramp.
Stamp, stampety, stamp, stamp.
(That's twice.)

Tramp, trampety, tramp, tramp.
Stamp, stampety, stamp, stamp.
(That's three times.)

Tramp, trampety, tramp, tramp.
Stamp, stampety, stamp, stamp.
(That's four times.)

Tramp, trampety, tramp, tramp.
Stamp, stampety, stamp, stamp.
(That's five times.)

Tramp, trampety, tramp, tramp.
Stamp, stampety, stamp, stamp.
(That's six times.)

Tramp, trampety, tramp, tramp.
Stamp, stampety, stamp, stamp.
(This is the seventh time.)

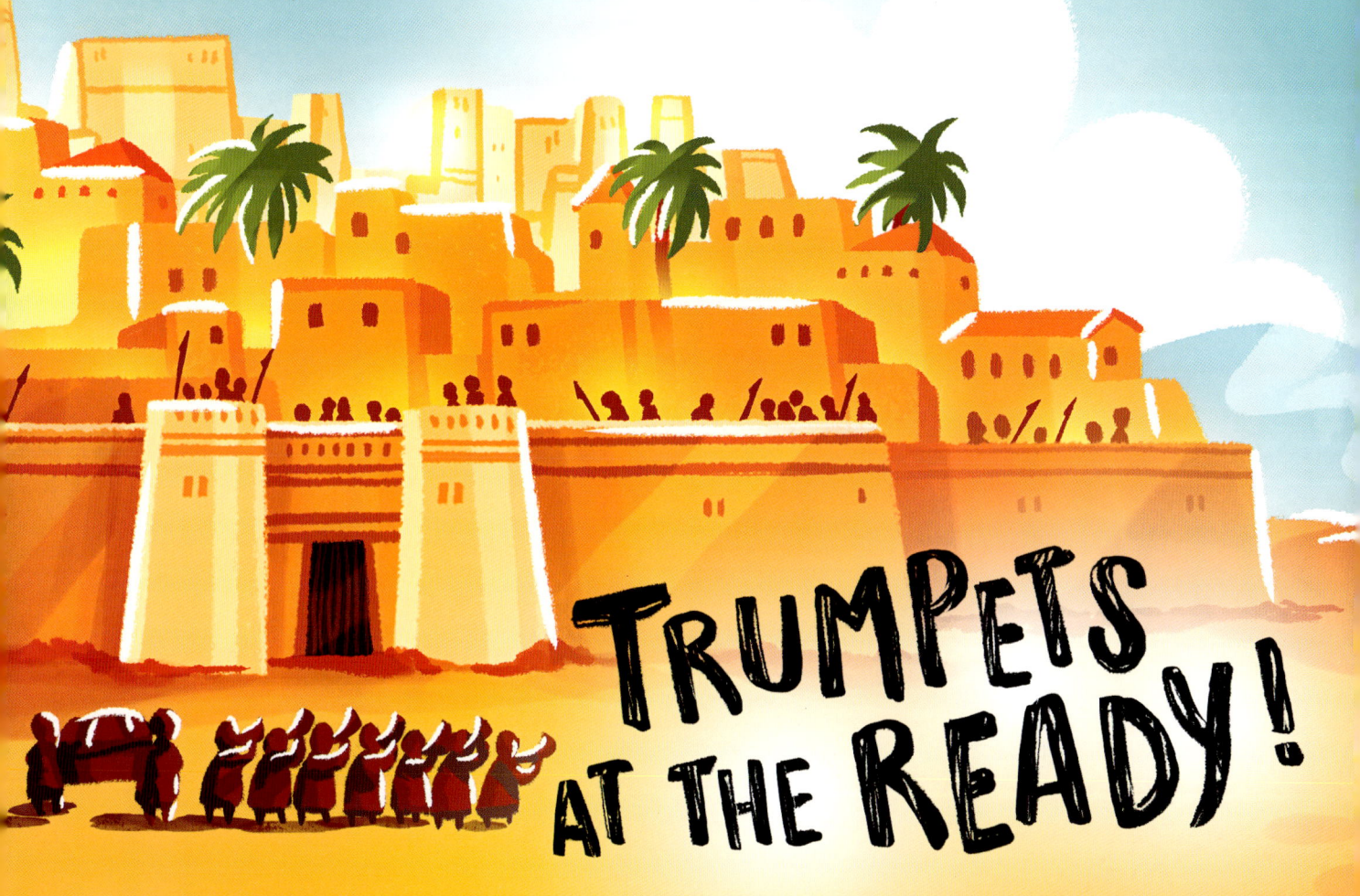

TRUMPETS AT THE READY!

Deep breath in and ready to shout...

And... SHOUT!

The walls cracked.

The walls crumbled.

And with a loud, crashing, smashing noise...

The walls of the Very Strong City came tumbling down.

The Very Mighty God had done what Joshua and the people couldn't do.

He smashed the big walls down. God was with his people.

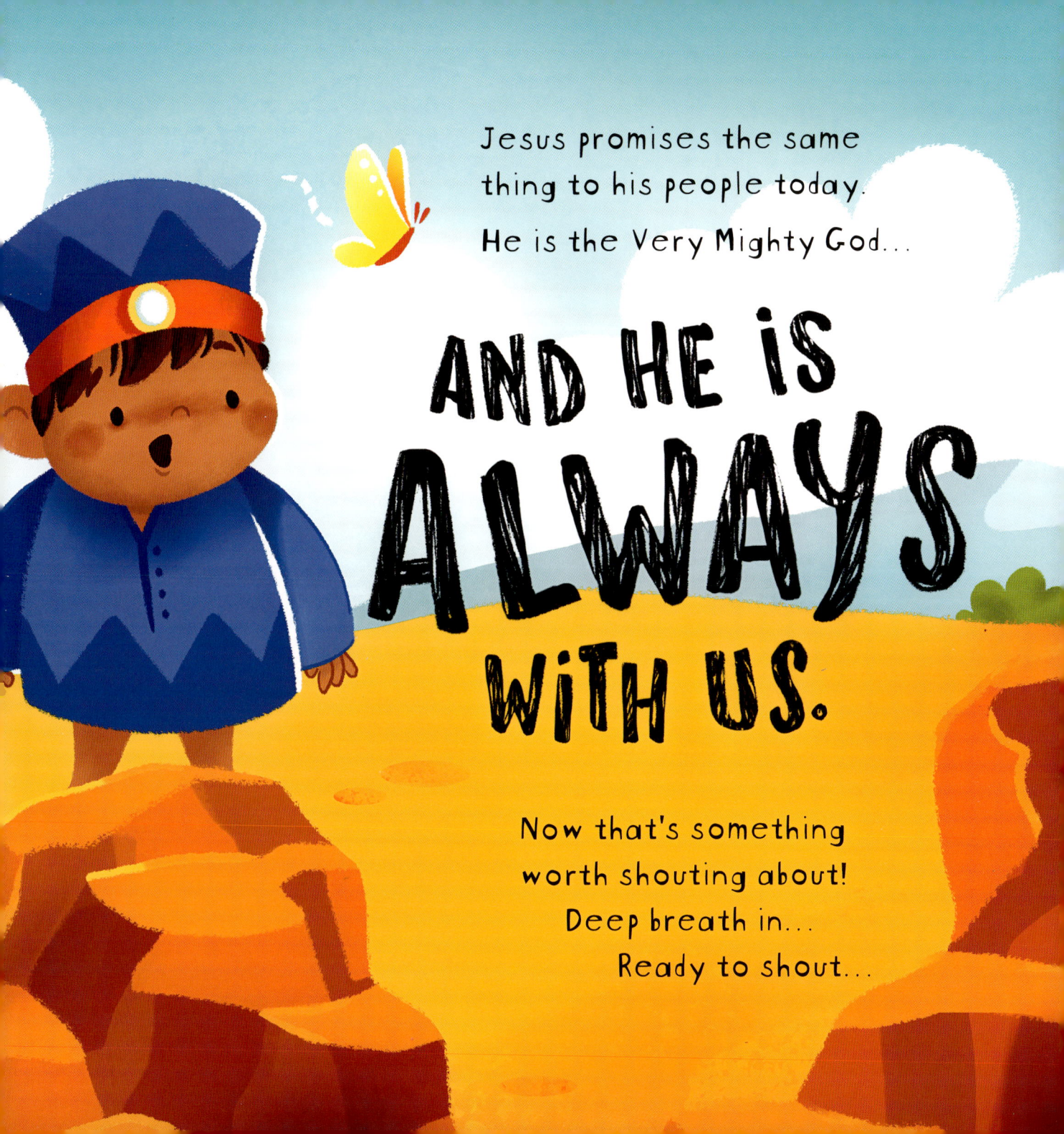

Jesus promises the same thing to his people today.

He is the Very Mighty God...

AND HE IS ALWAYS WITH US.

Now that's something worth shouting about!
Deep breath in...
Ready to shout...

Enjoy all of the Very Best Bible Stories Series:

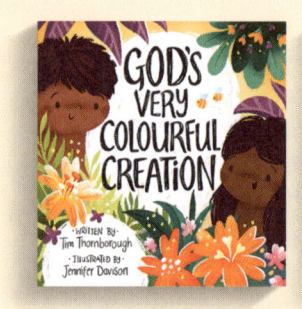 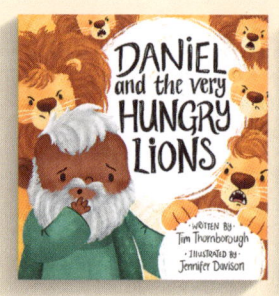 

 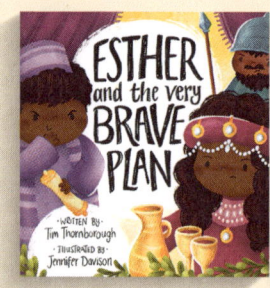 

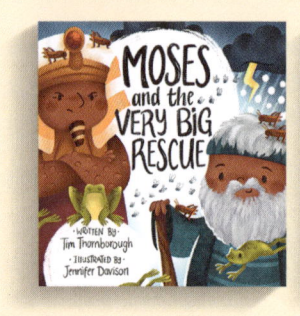 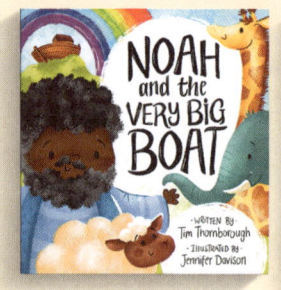 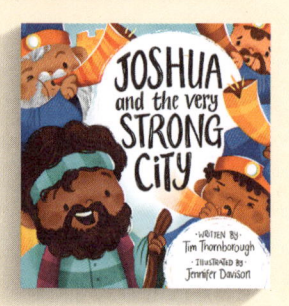

thegoodbook.com/vbbs | .co.uk/vbbs